MONICA PEDERSEN
MAKE IT BEAUTIFUL™

Stephanie's having a little girl.
little girl. little girl.
Stephanie's having a little girl
who will be dressed in pink & bows.

July 16, 2011

MONICA PEDERSEN
MAKE IT BEAUTIFUL
DESIGNS *and* IDEAS *for* ENTERTAINING *at* HOME

PHOTOGRAPHY BY PETER ROSENBAUM

MIDWAY

AN AGATE IMPRINT

CHICAGO

Printed in China.

First printing, January 2012
ISBN 978-1-57284-128-4

All photographs copyright © 2012 Peter Rosenbaum
Endpapers, Scalamandré.
Make It Beautiful is a registered trademark of Monica Pedersen.
Design by Brandtner Design.

10 11 12 13   10 9 8 7 6 5 4 3 2 1

Midway is an imprint of Agate Publishing. Agate books are available in bulk at discount prices. For more information, go to agatepublishing.com.

THIS BOOK IS DEDICATED TO
MY MOM AND DAD, FOR ALWAYS BEING AN INSPIRATION;
TO MY WONDERFUL HUSBAND, ERIK;
AND IN MEMORY OF MICHAEL AND MICHELE

Table of Contents

I LOVE TO DECORATE: my house, your house, back yard, front yard, and everything in between. When I was a designer on the HGTV design show *Designed to Sell*, my favorite day of every shoot week was our off-camera day, Friday. We spent it arranging, rearranging, hanging, removing, and pressing every textile to perfection. In less than one week's time, we finished projects that would normally have taken months to complete—and all for $2,000 or less. ❡ To answer a popular question, yes, our $2,000 budget was real. Fortunately, when it came to staying within budget, I had a secret weapon: my older sister, Michele. My design team referred to Michele as their honorary design assistant, and I called her my Garage Sale Girl. ❡ Michele had an inner GPS that always led her to the nearest garage sale. When our time and budget were both down to the wire, we'd call her up and send her on a shopping trip. Her charming ways and big personality enabled her to name

her price for whatever we needed. She can still be seen on *Designed to Sell* reruns during the open house segment, complimenting her little sister's work. If you happen to spot a curvy, six-foot-tall blonde who looks and sounds just like me, that's Michele.

My team and I filmed more than 90 episodes of *Designed to Sell*. Throughout our aggressive shoot schedule I had countless moments when my head was filled with thoughts anyone working on their home can relate to. *What do I do with this space? What will add the most value? How do I make it work within my budget? Can I get this project finished in time?*

When the answers to these questions just wouldn't come to me, I'd do the same thing I do when faced with these dilemmas in my design business and in my own home—hit the books. Design books and publications are where I look for inspiration.

While I've learned a ton from watching design shows (I'm especially susceptible to getting sucked in to *House Hunters* marathons on HGTV) and feel blessed to have such a wonderful job, to me, nothing is a more powerful design tool than a beautiful photograph that captures the look, feel, and detail of a space. Doing a design book of my own has been a longtime dream.

I'd been a print model for years, but when the design magazines and books started to outnumber the fashion magazines in my house, I knew it was time to hang up my pumps, and move on.

While I was working hard, taking any design job I could get, I eventually landed a national commercial for Sears in which I played the role of a housewife using her cordless drill while Bob Vila stood front and center talking tools. The commercial led to my audition for *Designed to Sell*. Never in a million years did I think I would get the job.

If you bought this book and are reading this right now, thank you! When I started to think about what type of book I'd want to do most, the answer was simple—entertaining. I've been decorating tables my whole life. Although I'm not a professional event planner, I've had the pleasure of designing many events for friends, family, and charities, as well as parties featured on *HGTV Dream Home* specials.

Whether I'm designing someone's home or just a table for a party, I'm answering the same questions: What is the right color, the right pattern, the right scale, the right function, and the right lighting? The way you consider the relationship of a new piece of furniture you're planning to introduce into a room to what is already in it is the same way you should look at designing a table for entertaining. Using your home's existing interior décor for inspiration and investing in versatile accessories are the keys to creating looks for entertaining that will work seamlessly in your home and work on any budget.

The lack of illustrations of place settings and formalities in this book is purely intentional. Who needs rules when you are having fun with friends and family? Good design is important to the way we live in our homes, of course, but when it comes to entertaining, it's all about making the effort. If your passion is cooking, start collecting recipes. If your passion is being a guest in the homes of others, be kind. But if your passion is design, pull out the china, embrace your style, and strut your stuff!

My favorite part of the entertaining process is creating the design. It's a passion I inherited from my mother, sparked by some inspiration from a copy of a now-out-of-print design magazine called *Southern Accents* (I miss it so) that arrived in my mailbox in January 2001.

At that time, my husband Erik and I had just moved in to our first house, a charming English Tudor built in 1928. On the outside, it looked like a gingerbread house, and on the inside, it was like the set of a bad seventies movie. The only thing missing was a mirrored disco ball. While I was busy both tearing apart and defending my moneypit of a home and its "good bones", I began to lose faith that I'd ever get to the point where I could stop renovating and start decorating.

At the moment that particular issue of *Southern Accents* arrived, I was just about to begin sanding the drywall in my guest bathroom—at my father's insistence—and welcome carpenters in my house to tear out the existing Lucite staircase to be replaced by something more appropriate for the house. In a desperate effort to take a break from the dust and noise around me, I retreated to the master bedroom to relax in the best way I know how—sitting down and reading a design magazine.

The magazine's cover featured a bedroom designed around a gorgeous cream and sage toile patterned wallpaper and fabric. I instantly fell in love with the look. As I flipped through the pages and saw the rest of the rooms in the home, I realized that I'd suddenly found some much-needed inspiration and direction for the design of my home. Years later, I met two of the magazine's gifted editors, Frances MacDougall and Karen Carroll. They graciously arranged a meeting so that I could personally tell the home's Atlanta-based designer, Dan Carithers, how much his work had influenced my career.

The way colors and patterns were introduced into each room in the home I saw in the pages of *Southern Accents* reminded me very much of how my greatest influence of all—my mom—had decorated her home. While my mother was always on a tight budget, she spent wisely, buying only what she loved and what for her would pay off the most in terms of the overall design scheme—yards and yards of beautiful fabric.

Just as my mother had done before me, all of my designs use fabric as a starting point. Since the idea of—or space for—a craft room didn't exist for our family, my mother's sewing machine had a permanent spot at our kitchen table. While my twin brother Michael and I did our homework, she sat beside us with her foot to the pedal, producing curtains, bedspreads, pillow shams, clothing, Halloween costumes, and, of course, tableskirts. I cannot remember a single day from my childhood where there was not a tableskirt on our kitchen table. My mother's tableskirts typically touched the floor and were often finished with a two-inch box pleat or gathered ruffle along the hem. One of my greatest regrets is that I have few pictures of her creations—just memories.

In addition to her love of using whatever she could get her hands on as a tableskirt, my mother loved all things tabletop. Our cabinets were always bursting at the seams with teapots, cups, saucers, china, and napkin rings—you name it, she had options!

Our shared birthday was the one time of the year when she encouraged my brother and me to join her in her tabletop design endeavors. Birthdays are a big deal when you're a twin! In an effort to help us express our individual identities—a common desire of parents of twins—she gave each of us our own birthday cake to decorate. Michael and I went to town decorating large rectangular sheet cakes from Sara Lee! Michael usually had to make several trips to the hobby store for Hot Wheels stuff or G.I. Joe figures before he was satisfied with his cake. Predictably, I stuck with dollhouse miniature furnishings, ballerinas, or flowers.

One year, I decided to be ultracreative with my blank birthday canvas—I wrote the birthday message on my cake in uncooked alphabet noodles. The result? Not pretty, and not fun to bite into! It was the first of many crafts-gone-bad moments for me. If you're a crafter, you know what I mean...not sweating design disasters and kitchen mishaps is the key to enjoying entertaining. Every great host has an equally great horror story.

We handled decorating the cakes, and my mother would always make sure there was a fresh, new tableskirt on the table. The look was finished by the gift I always asked of my godmother, Mary Ellen—a bouquet of white daisies. For me, the decorated table was all the present I needed.

My mother was always busy balancing work, motherhood, being a wife, and working hard to make all of the events in our household special, but in reality, she was doing much more than that. She was creating memories and traditions to be enjoyed and passed down.

I've styled the photos and short stories in this book in order to make you feel like you are sitting at the table as my guest. Join me for fun, inspiring designs and beautiful memories in the pages of this book. And remember—whatever you choose to celebrate, make the effort, enjoy the process, and make it beautiful, on any budget. It's worth it! ✦

Black and White Baby Shower

Stephanie's having a little girl.
little girl. little girl.
Stephanie's having a little girl
who will be dressed in pink & bows.

My Porch Is Your Porch

O NE OF MY DEAREST FRIENDS has a lovely tradition. Every summer, she opens her porch to family and friends for what she calls "porch time." After I'd told her for perhaps the thousandth time how much I love the lighting on the porch—I know a great white sweep when I see one—my friend offered me the use of her porch for one of my parties. I jumped at the chance! ¶ My dear friend and modeling agent Stephanie and I had been trying for some time to get together and celebrate her first pregnancy. As her due date drew near and we canceled yet another planned lunch date, I told her that the only way we'd be sure to get a date for the shower on the books before the baby was born was to literally put it, in the form of a baby shower for her, in this book! I contacted some mutual friends and we got to work planning a fun and beautiful shower for Stephanie. We picked a date and I put my design plan into action.

There was a time in my life when I felt like I was either hosting or attending a baby shower every weekend! I decided to learn from the past and change my approach. Instead of blowing my whole design budget on baby-themed accessories, I decided to spend the majority of it on design items that would look great in the same space long after the shower was over. After all, having guests over is a great motivator and a great excuse to get one's house decorated.

FIRST, THE STYLE

Now, back to the porch. Secretly, I had always longed to accessorize my friend's beautiful porch with one of my favorite black and white fabrics, Scalamandré's Zebra. Now that the shower was coming up, I was thrilled to have the perfect excuse to do it! The bold, lively, and large-scale print would be a festive way to greet the guests and at the same time, it would beautifully complement the existing black-and-white color scheme of the porch.

I ordered ten yards of the fabric and made a quick stop at the upholsterer to give him directions for fabricating pillowcovers and a tableskirt. Since the pattern's repeat is quite large both vertically and horizontally, I decided to drape two pieces of the fabric in three-yard lengths over a forty-two-inch round table, which seats four to six comfortably and allows for both intimate and animated conversation. The plan looked fantastic and didn't compromise the beauty of the pattern. Doing so also saved money—opting to have the edges hemmed rather than paying for a custom tableskirt was considerably less expensive. Now that I have these lovely finished three-yard lengths of the fabric, I'm finding that it was an even better investment than I'd thought. I can reuse these lengths on a rectangular table, which will beautifully show off the stunning vertical repeat.

One of the bonuses of using black and white as a baby shower design theme is that both colors look great paired with pinks, blues, and even yellow and green if the baby's gender is unknown. Since Stephanie was having a girl, pale pink it would be! Since

the porch was stunning on its own, my shopping list to pull together this great look was short and simple:

- *Pale pink satin ribbon.*
- *Black and white card stock for menu cards.*
- *An order with a local florist for four dozen pale pink roses to match the ribbon (I made sure to bring a sample of the ribbon to the florist so he could match the color of the roses to it).*
- *Cardboard letters to be painted pink.*
- *Small white gift bags for party favors.*
- *A fun stamp to play up the animal print and baby theme.*
- *A set of five small cosmetic brushes from Chanel to be given as favors. The free gift wrap that Chanel offers at its counters allowed me to take something off of my to-do list — always welcome when planning a party!*

I also engaged an artist to create a personalized chalkboard that served as artwork for the party and would later hang in Stephanie's nursery.

Because I was hosting a party in someone else's home and wanted to make as little impact as possible, I brought everything in I would need, including six place settings of inexpensive white china, pretty stemware, and elegant flatware. Napkins were a snap—I had some of the extra fabric lined with poplin.

Many stores that carry tabletop accessories offer affordable catering kits with prices that are comparable to renting. Buying one set—or several—can be a great investment if you do a lot of entertaining outside of your home. White dinnerware works with every design plan.

To make things easy for myself, I picked up a catered lunch from the English Room at the Deer Path Inn: Classic Bruschetta and a Grilled Chicken Salad with Pears, Gorgonzola, and Balsamic Vinegar (see recipes on page 182). One of my favorite nearby bakeries, the Bent Fork, made the beautiful, simple, and delicious chocolate two-layer cake with white icing. I love this cake anyway, but I also knew that once it had been sliced, the contrast between the dark cake and white icing would look really fun with the rest of the design. The guest of honor enjoyed her cake with milk, while the rest of us shared a bottle of Moscato from a winemaker called Seven Daughters. I had a great time working the daughter theme into as many aspects of the party as I could!

While catching up was certainly on the to-do list for the partygoers, I also wanted to incorporate a couple of fun baby shower games, which are especially fun when guests don't know each other well.

Stephanie had measured our waistlines for years when we were her models, so now it was time to turn the tables—and measure her growing waistline. Once we had our guesses on paper, I measured her waistline with some extra satin ribbon and then laid the ribbon alongside my tape measure. The winner? Our friend Eleanor—being the mother of four kids herself definitely gave her the advantage!

The next game we played is my absolute favorite: Name That Baby. On the invitation, I'd asked each guest to bring a baby picture of herself. I gathered together the ladies' photos, randomly assigned numbers to each of them, and then asked the girls to match each number with the correct girl's name. This game is especially fun for a couples baby shower, because it can be hard to tell baby boys and girls apart!

The great setting, beautiful design, fantastic food, and good friends made it a memorable day for all of us. We sent a very pregnant Stephanie on her way home; the rest of us stayed well into the evening, until the porch lights went off. ✦

Audrey was born on August 19, 2011. She was six pounds and five ounces of baby girl. Congratulations, Stephanie, on the birth of your beautiful daughter.

Have fun carrying the color scheme into the dessert course, as with this Black and White Buttercream Zebra Cake.

Stephanie's having a little girl.
little girl. little girl.
Stephanie's having a little girl
who will be dressed in pink & bows.

July 15, 2001

If you're hosting an outdoor baby shower during the summer months, it's a good idea to keep a fan on hand for your pregnant guest of honor.

Eco-Friendly Graduation Party

Going Green Is Gorgeous!

WHEN IT COMES TO A GRADUATION PARTY, it's all about the graduate! In this case, I was very lucky. The graduate was a very special girl named Charlotte. She's six feet tall, super beautiful, super smart, super sweet, and super talented to boot. ❡ Charlotte is the daughter of a very good friend of mine and has a passion for photography. In fact, she became my photography intern while I worked on this book. At one of our earliest meetings, I mentioned to Charlotte that I'd planned to include a graduation party that reflected eco-friendly design. Charlotte loved the idea and offered up her own graduation party for me, as she shares her family's passion for environmentally friendly living. After speaking with Charlotte's mom, a Chicago interior designer and tastemaker, I had my marching orders: The graduation party,

with a guest list of forty, would have an elegant but casual tone. Charlotte and I agreed that sending paperless invitations would perfectly echo the "green" theme.

Now that the eco-friendly theme had been established, Charlotte and I focused on the location and design plan. I knew we had to find a location that would also have a nearby backup indoor location in case of bad weather. With that in mind, we spent the day scouting locations.

After considering many options, my graduate finally came clean about her true wish. Charlotte wanted to have her party near the barn where she had spent much of her childhood riding horses. Not having grown up around horses myself, I was a bit hesitant about this idea. Charlotte convinced me to tour the area, and seeing the barn's setup and watching my graduate with her horses put my fears to rest. We decided on the perfect location—a beautiful spot under a row of mature walnut trees, just along the horse fence. This setting was magical to behold and would provide a bit of shelter from the sun and any unforeseen rain showers that might pop up.

We decided to seat our forty guests at a single long table under the walnut trees. We rented eight thirty-inch-wide by eight-foot-long tables and set them up, two abreast, to create a sixty-inch-wide table that was an impressive thirty-two feet long! For the tableskirt, I chose an oversized sage green buffalo check fabric called Gertrude's Rose. I have always loved this pattern, especially in this particular green colorway, and in step with the eco-friendly theme, the fabric was 100 percent cotton. The fabric's directional pattern looked beautiful running parallel to the lines of the horse fence, and the busy, oversized buffalo check created an intimate feel for our very long table. Charlotte loved the hip look of the randomly scattered roses.

The fabric's soft shades of green, gray, and white were the inspiration for the centerpieces and tabletop accessories. The centerpieces consisted of six large floral arrangements that were accompanied by smaller satellite arrangements scattered along the length of the table. The flowers were a mix of white roses, lilies, and freshly picked hydrangeas that came from the farm's garden. Random greenery was added as filler. Since weather can be unpredictable, we created the centerpieces the night before and kept them in a cool spot.

Charlotte's mother was out antiquing one day and sent me a picture snapped on her cell phone of fifty antique wooden folding chairs—originally schoolhouse chairs from Sweden—that were in perfect condition. Buying the chairs would actually be less expensive than renting, and giving antiques new life would help drive home the green message of repurposing and renewing. I quickly texted back: "Grab them!" Best of all, the chairs would be used again and again for future parties.

The last design item to consider was the lighting. The party would start at 6 p.m., so the lighting had to look fabulous and be functional into the evening. I reached out to my friend Melissa Edelman, who owns one of my favorite antique stores, Antiquaire, and asked if I could borrow a couple of the beautiful chandeliers I had seen hanging in her shop's windows. I left her store with two nine-light, vintage, Italian wooden chandeliers that looked gorgeous hanging from branches of the walnut tree.

For the food, we reached out to an amazing organic farm, Tempel Farms Organics. I have long appreciated the farm's stands at farmers markets in downtown Chicago and the northern suburbs. (For recipes by Peggy Markel, see page 183.) We paired the food with a Sauvignon Blanc and a Merlot provided by the classic Napa Valley vineyard Rutherford Hill, which pioneered the California Merlot.

At the end of this lovely evening, I presented Charlotte with a personalized book filled with words of wisdom from her guests. The guests did not leave empty handed, either, as linen-wrapped red oak seedlings were passed out as party favors. We asked that our guests plant their seedlings and allow them to grow along with our special graduate. ✦

Beet Salad with pine nuts & goat cheese
on a bed of organic greens

Organic Asparagus Salad mixed with
red & yellow peppers, drizzled with a tarragon vinaigrette

Roasted Baby Potatoes

Orzo with organic heirloom tomatoes

Organic Chicken sauteed in
fresh herb & brown butter sauce

If you do a lot of entertaining, invest in versatile glass accessories. Clear glass matches everything! Repurposing these glass candleholders as floral containers was an easy way to keep in step with the green theme of this party.

TEMPEL FARMS ORGANICS

FARMERS

MARKET

OPEN

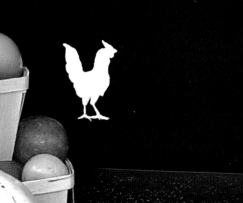

Enhance the farm to table experience
by decorating your table with beautiful food,
served family style.

Always check with the guest of honor before the party to make sure you're not planning to wear the same dress that she plans to wear, especially if she's a bit younger than you are.

At the end of this lovely evening, I presented Charlotte with a personalized book filled with words of wisdom from her guests.

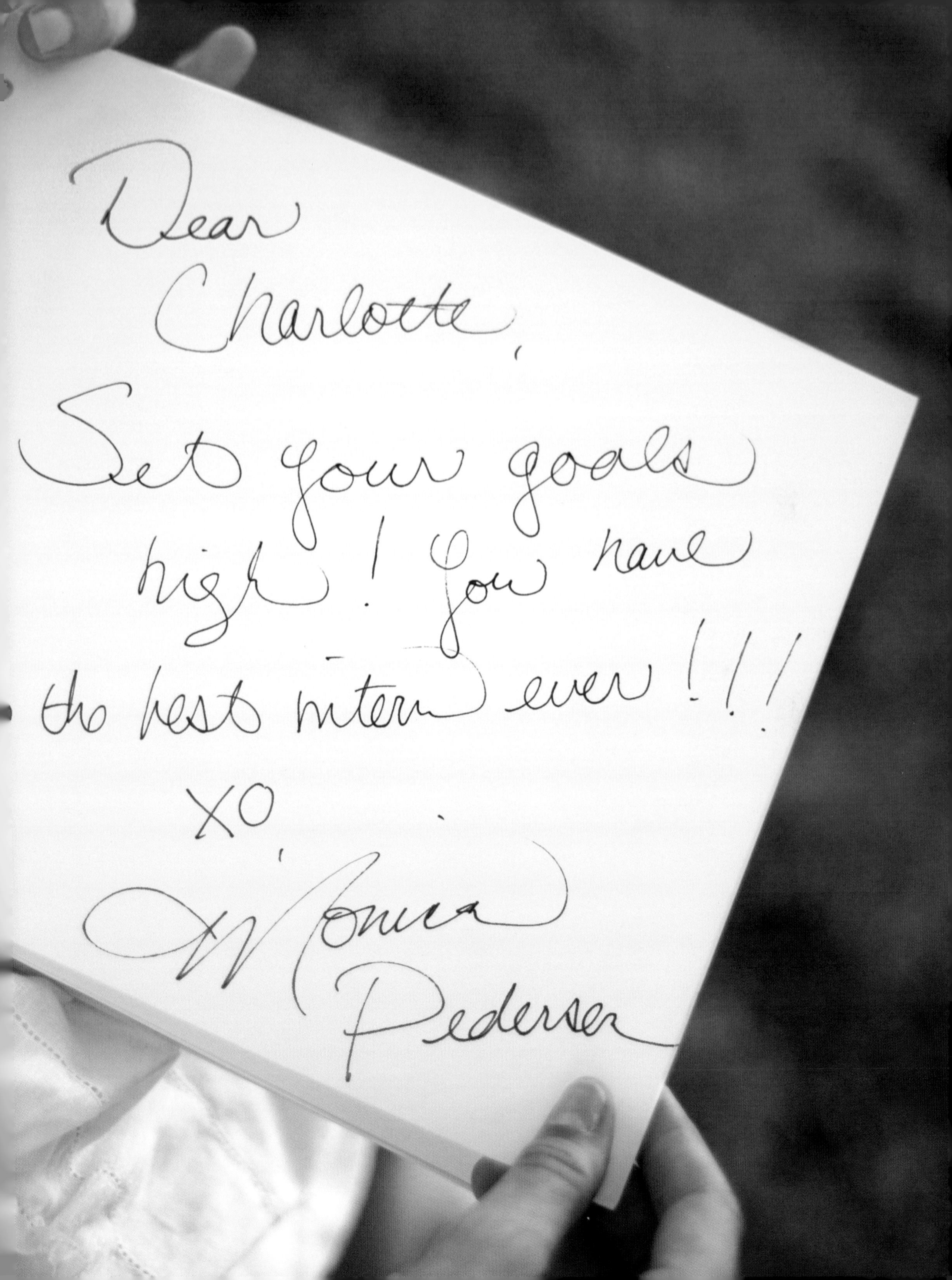

Dear
Charlotte,
Set your goals
high! You have
the best intern ever!!!
XO
Monica
Pedersen

The Perfect Wedding

It's All About the Bride

MY FIRST MISSION IN DESIGNING this wedding party was to inspire all those stressed-out brides-to-be out there—girls, you know you are out there. I know from my own experience exactly how overwhelming design choices can be when you're planning a wedding. Years ago, my husband Erik and I had a lovely winter wedding designed with layers of white and a long guest list. It was beautiful, but deep down I still had a longing for a small summer wedding reception. The look and setting for this party is exactly the look I would plan if Erik and I were to do it all over again—both elegant and intimate!   Mission number two was to design a tablescape with a fabric I had been fantasizing about for a long time: Scalamandré's Kilfane. I used Kilfane when decorating a guest bedroom once and was thrilled with the

You can make your wedding beautiful on any budget.

elegant feeling it created in the room. I knew the gorgeous damask fabric would look fantastic as a tableskirt for a wedding.

The small-scale candelabras looked elegant and unpretentious. The table flowers and bridal bouquet were simple as well. All it took were a few inexpensive silverplate mint julep cups, which make for versatile tabletop accessories in many party situations, and four dozen ivory roses. Dressing up the basic three-tier wedding cake and the cake table with extra roses meant adding lots of style without spending lots of money. The smoky look of the votive candles scattered on the table blended the mix of shiny and tarnished silvers.

I rented dinnerware with glass chargers, knowing they would allow the pattern of the beautiful Kilfane to show through. I picked up the Josair crystal stemware and grand baroque silverware at a fabulous antique store, Ivy & Co. I also rented Chiavari-style chairs in ivory that matched both the restrained color palette and the lovely architectural details of the covered porch.

Designing this party also gave me an excuse to pull out my wedding dress. It doesn't quite fit me like it used to, but it fit our model, the lovely Sophia, perfectly. Unfortunately, the "groom" I had booked for the shoot ended up standing up my "bride"—he backed out at the last minute. In the end, gorgeous Sophia stole the show anyway, because let's face it—weddings are all about the bride.

I couldn't have been happier with the way this perfect, small summer wedding turned out. In fact, the only things keeping me from taking advantage of the setting personally were my priest and my husband. ✦

When designing
with a neutral palette,
incorporate a variety
of patterns and
textures to create
a layered look.

*Don't be
afraid
to mix
polished
and
tarnished
silvers.*

Whether you are
designing for
your home or for
a rented venue,
look to architectural
details for inspiration.
Always keep the
"where" in mind
when making
design decisions.

Add a lot of style
without spending
a lot of money by
dressing up your
wedding cake and
table with roses.

Tea for Two

"O, Canada! Our Home and..."

O F ALL OF THE PARTIES IN THIS BOOK, "Tea for Two" was my favorite, both to design and also to enjoy. Those who know me well know that I talk about my mom often, particularly in the context of what an inspiration she has been for me, and how much respect I have for her. Everything about the way I design has a bit of my mom in it—to name just one, watching my mother make countless beautiful tableskirts over the years directly influenced my personal passion for designing around fabrics. ¶ More important, I truly enjoy spending time with my mother. We both feel very fortunate that we've always had such a great relationship. However, as close as we are, there is one thing we don't agree on. While my mother inherited her own mother's obsession with all things pertaining to tea—everything from the endless varieties of tea itself to collecting beautiful teacups and teapots—somehow, with me, it skipped a generation. I drink coffee. But when I'm with my mom, I drink tea.

Because I know my mother so well, styling this party was beyond easy. I knew she'd love a colorful, patterned tableskirt, preferably with a pop of red. My mom has often talked about how much she loves the energy that red accents can bring into the home. Her love of red most likely was born from her Maple Leaf beginnings (she is Canadian). I'm sure that her childhood spent in the Commonwealth has much to do with her love of tea.

For the tableskirt, I chose a fabric with a pattern that reminded me of many of the charming tableskirts my mother uses in her own home. I used beautiful embroidered linen napkins I'd bought years ago in Ireland on a trip my mom and I had taken with Erik. To add a bit more of my mother's signature red to the table, I placed red tea roses in small pewter containers. I made a makeshift tea caddy by selecting a lovely wooden antique box from Erik's extensive collection.

As for the menu, I stuck with tradition. I served orange pekoe tea, my mother's favorite. To satisfy her sweet tooth, I served shortbread cookies and Lemon Squares made with her special recipe (see recipe on page 185).

My mother is the most unpretentious and unfussy person in the world—but she does observe a few rules when enjoying her tea. As in, "Dear, you really should use a teapot rather than a coffeepot when serving tea." "Dear, the Lemon Squares need to be on a paper doily." I knew I'd missed a big one when she asked, "Where are your sugar cube tongs?" As usual, I can't slip anything past her.

I'm so grateful that I have the photos and memories of this beautiful afternoon with my mother. Once my mom had finished the Tea Party 101 class, we went back to doing what we do best—drinking tea, enjoying each other's company, and, of course, adoring her precious dog, Henry, who as usual was sitting at her feet. ◆

My mother's love of sweets is matched only by her skills in the kitchen. I highly recommend trying her recipe for Lemon Squares on page 185. The first time my mom made this recipe, she and I just about finished off the whole pan.

Coffee and...

The Art of Staging

THIS WAS A PARTY my photographer, Peter, and I designed and photographed before we started working on *MAKE IT BEAUTIFUL*. "Coffee and..." is a phrase that both our mothers used often when extending casual invitations to friends. I cannot speak for Peter's mom, Marcia, but I can say that my mother meant coffee and...some amazing sweet that she had baked herself. ¶ In order to make things easy, we set up the shoot in Peter's kitchen and pulled props from our own personal collections. (Peter's orange-banded china from Fitz and Floyd is also featured in the Book Club party on page 130.) I approached this party the same way I would approach a design plan for HGTV's *Designed to Sell*: keeping costs low by introducing details that would have the most impact. As usual, I chose to carry this out by using beautiful fabric. On the day of our shoot, I pulled out my sewing machine and tool bag and enlisted the help of one of my very special design assistants, Leslie Weiner. Leslie and I quickly sewed floor-length draperies and napkins out of extra fabric that I'd brought from my home. We found it very easy to work with the stripe and luxurious weight of the linen.

Next, Leslie and I hung artwork on the walls by one of my favorite artists, Lupus Garrett Lupus. We dressed the table with a runner crafted out of a one-and-a-half–yard remnant of a coordinating paisley fabric. The orange and beige colorway of these fabrics looked fantastic in Peter's kitchen.

For the tabletop accessories, we mixed Peter's Fitz and Floyd china with inexpensive orange accent plates I'd picked up on clearance the day before. Never hesitate to mix fine and not-so-fine china on your table!

I used Peter's gorgeous William Yeoward goblets to put my own spin on "Coffee and…" For my friends, it's coffee and… mimosas. Feminine centerpieces of orange roses in silver bowls finished the look and provided contrast with the rustic table and contemporary Mario Bellini Cab chairs.

Our "Coffee and…" day was a blast. It made us even more excited than ever to embark on *Make It Beautiful*! ◆

Wine and Design

Stags Leap Style

A WINE-TASTING PARTY CAN BE ONE OF THE EASIEST, most enjoyable, and most affordable parties to host. It is a perfect theme for a holiday open house, office party, or impromptu get-together with friends. Best of all, a wine tasting requires very little work ahead of time. ¶ There are a number of formats for a wine tasting party, including: a vertical wine tasting, which involves tasting different vintages of the same wine from the same winery; a horizontal wine tasting, where all of the wines are from the same vintage but different wineries; or a general wine tasting, where you set your own criteria, price range, region, varietals, and so on. The wine-tasting party I decided to host was a general tasting that would allow me to feature wines from one of my favorite wine regions, the Stags Leap district of Napa Valley in California.

Given the region's history and reputation, I knew a Stags Leap tasting would be memorable in terms of the fantastic wines, and that my guests would also find it educational. During a 1976 blind tasting held in Paris (known as the "Judgment of Paris") of American and French wines, a 1973 Stag's Leap Wine Cellars Cabernet Sauvignon was awarded first place by nine French judges, an American judge, and the Brit who organized the tasting, wine merchant Steven Spurrier. (The Stag's Leap vineyard uses an apostrophe in "Stag's," while the district does not.) The wine world was shocked that French producers such as Mouton-Rothschild and Haut Brion were topped by a California wine, but the Judgment of Paris irrevocably placed the Stags Leap district on the map as one the greatest producers of Cabernet Sauvignon in the world.

Frontmost in my mind as I styled this party was introducing textures and colors that reflected Napa style while keeping the wine front and center. I chose to go with slipcovered furnishings in a natural linen color to reflect the ease and laidback look of Napa style (and here's the bonus: the slipcovers could be easily cleaned in case of a wine spill). The dis-

tressed table mimicked the look and feel of an old wine barrel, and the wines were separated by rustic wooden trays with iron handles. Dark iron candlesticks grounded the look, and small containers of orchids reflected the rich colors of the wines.

The place settings included chargers with an ikat print. Normally, I would say that charger plates are a bit too formal for this kind of party, but these ikat chargers were so fabulous on the table I just couldn't resist pulling them out of my inventory. (Never be afraid to break design rules in the name of beauty!) I paired the chargers with antique plates featuring a hunt scene that I had borrowed from my friend, who also happens to share my addiction to beautiful china. I'm certain that at some point our families will be staging a china intervention.

Carefully organizing the wines' presentation is always a good idea. For obvious reasons, it's easy to mix up the glasses after you've had a few too many sips. The shape of the wine glasses, which are made by Riedel, lent a graceful look to the table and are engineered to enhance the experience of tasting wines. A staple for serious wine drinkers, Riedel glassware is a great investment. You can find it at most stores that carry tabletop accessories.

Natural horn-handled silverware and cheese servers added to the casual, layered look, and a scattering of a few stag horns finished off the theme of the tablescape.

Alongside each table setting, I placed a small leather notebook for guests to use as a wine journal during the party. Recording your personal thoughts about wines, their pairings, and the characteristics you like and dislike in wines is an easy way to start building your personal knowledge of wines. A wine journal notebook should be small enough to fit into a man's suitcoat pocket or a woman's evening bag, so you can also bring them along to a restaurant or store to help take the guesswork out of selecting wines you're sure to enjoy.

I also made a simple linen bow to dress up each journal and secure to it a corkscrew that was included as a favor. I wrapped the same linen that was used for the bow around an inch-thick piece of Styrofoam placed inside the tray to ensure a perfectly even surface for the wine bottles and stemware.

Crackers, baguettes, fig spread, dried apricots, and a variety of cheddar cheeses from Kerrygold paired beautifully with the different Cabernet Sauvignons we poured. (Janet Fletcher wrote a terrific book on wine and cheese pairings called *Cheese & Wine: A Guide to Selecting, Pairing, and Enjoying*—read it, and you'll never be caught wondering what cheese goes with what wine again!)

The tasting was a wonderful success. The beautiful setting and special guests made tasting a wonderful collection of wines from the Stags Leap district even more delicious—and who knew that was even possible? If you love good wine and can't get to Napa Valley, bring a little bit of Napa into your own home by hosting a Stags Leap district wine tasting party. ✦

Since the aroma of wine is such an important part of the wine-tasting experience, skip the fragrant candles and use only flowers that do not have a scent. Orchids are a good choice.

At each table setting, I placed
a small leather notebook for guests
to use as a wine journal during
the party, and to take home as a gift.

The setting and guests made tasting a wonderful collection of wines from the Stags Leap district even more delicious — who knew that was even possible?

That's Italian

Have Tableskirt, Will Travel!

M**Y HUSBAND AND I COMPLETELY AGREE** about three of our favorite things: favorite ethnic food (Italian), favorite TV show (*Top Chef*), and favorite contestant on *Top Chef* (Fabio Viviani). Erik and I are definitely wannabe Italians…our best friends in Chicago are Italian, and we were first introduced many years ago by a mutual friend, an Italian chef named Luigi Negroni. You get the picture. ¶ Since I am such a huge Fabio fan, I was thrilled to have the chance to meet him in Chicago at the annual Chicago Gourmet event. He and I were both there working for the Terlato Wine Group—I was talking about wine and design, and Fabio was there to talk about food and wine pairings. If you have seen Fabio before on TV, you know that he is talented, kind, charming, and most of all, hilarious. People flock to him naturally, and at Chicago Gourmet, it was great fun to watch how he made each fan he talked to feel special.

Since that first meeting, Fabio repeatedly invited Erik and I to dine with him at his restaurant, Café Firenze, the next time we visited L.A. Unfortunately, we could never seem to get our schedules together. Eventually, I found the perfect opportunity.

I called Fabio and asked if I could take advantage of his generous invitation—with a twist. I was about to host the *HGTV Halloween Block Party* special with Design Star Antonio Ballatore in L.A., so I asked if I could host a party for a few of my friends at Café Firenze. The guest list included my booking agent, Bethany Dick; Peter Rosenbaum, my photographer extraordinare; Antonio; and Fabio himself!

Ever the gracious restaurateur, Fabio quickly replied, "Anything you need! Come on by." My only challenge was to figure out how I was going to design this dinner party from a few thousand miles away!

My first thoughts went to the tableskirt. My good friend at Scalamandré, Peter Julian, helped me pick out an authentic Italian printed fabric—Stravagante, a gorgeous fruit-and-floral print taken from the archives of the Medici family. I loved the pattern's history, and I knew the colorful, appetizing pattern would complement Fabio's menu and the Italian theme of my dinner party. So I packed the tableskirt into my luggage and took off for sunny L.A.

THE PARTY DAY APPROACHES

With Peter in tow, I was off to host, shop, and prop. Since I had no idea what the dinnerware in Fabio's restaurant looked like, I decided to rent most of the party's tabletop accessories, with one exception—a set of gorgeous floral pasta bowls with a pop of cobalt blue that were supplied by my china-loving photographer, Peter.

Finding accessories was easy! I was in the hometown of one of the most famous prop houses in the world, L.A.'s Omega Cinema Props, where I found myself shopping alongside some of the most talented set stylists in both TV and film. At Omega, I was especially thrilled to find bamboo-handled silverware, since the Scalamandré fabric I'd chosen reminded me of a vintage pattern that Gucci once featured on scarves and bamboo-handled handbags. I easily and quickly found all the accessories I was looking for, and the great staff at Omega expedited my order so I could get to the restaurant to set up.

As usual, Fabio had a full reservation sheet for the night, so I set up outside and took advantage of Café Firenze's beautiful patio. Fabio's equally charming business partner, Jacopo Falleni, warmly encouraged us to make ourselves comfortable. I layered the table with vivid, colorful floral arrangements, lots of fresh produce, and loads of candlesticks.

We all enjoyed Fabio's amazing food: gnocchi, Burrata cheese, and prosciutto wrapped prawns (you can find the recipe for his gnocchi on page 186). We hadn't been at the table long before I knew my guests would be hanging out late into the night,

After a few bottles of Chianti, and in typical Italian fashion, we created memories and made new friends while enjoying great food. I left L.A. full of thoughts of what Chicago was missing: a restaurant for Fabio, an episode of a show for me to shoot with Antonio, and a cool tattoo for me, too. (Just kidding!) By the way, the Halloween special in L.A. was a competition, and of course, Antonio won by a landslide! ✦

Book Club

Chez Rosenbaum

WHEN MY GOOD FRIEND, photographer Peter Rosenbaum, asked me to style a small gathering at his home for our book club, I was thrilled. He and I met many years ago, when I was a print model and he was a fashion photographer. In the early days of our friendship, we made a habit of retreating to his library to pore over fashion photography. In more recent years, our shared library time has been more focused on studying photography of a different kind—that of food and interiors. ¶ In addition to being a well-known photographer, Peter has also earned an excellent reputation for his talents in the kitchen. Whenever my husband is asked to recommend the best restaurant in Chicago, he replies, "Chez Rosenbaum," and gives Peter's home address. (This has probably confused a lot of people.)

Styling a party in his library was going to be fun, for sure, but it also made me a little nervous. Peter's epitomizes style and his approval means a lot to me. Everything he touches looks flawless. His studio's interior design, the way he sets the table for lunch, or the way he grabs clothes from the on-set stylist and tweaks them to perfection—Peter is always right. My mother often says, "That Peter! He can do anything!" (I agree!)

I wanted to create a look for Peter that I knew he would enjoy. What better way, I thought, than to use accessories he loves from his own home? "Borrowing" his own belongings from other places in the house also made things very convenient—I could just pull from his endless collection of beautiful china, crystal, and silver.

The only design purchases I had to make were fabric for the custom tableskirt, the napkins, and the flowers for the table. I selected a classic paisley pattern for the tableskirt called Highland Fling. The richness of the fabric blended beautifully with the library's architectural details, the handsome wood floor, and the rich wall color. I had napkins made from chocolate brown velvet lined with brown cotton poplin.

The afternoon of our book club party, I shopped Peter's collections and chose some white china from Fitz and Floyd with an orange band. The pieces looked terrific with Peter's gold salt and pepper shakers from Pickard. The antique crystal wine glasses I selected had been his grandmother's, and the water glasses originally held candles from a French company called Cire Trudon, the world's oldest candlemaking company.

I found a couple of bronze elephant bookends on a library shelf and a few candlesticks and worked them into the tablescape. Since the tarnish on the candlesticks looked great with the fabric, I skipped giving them a quick polish. If an accessory looks good on the table, use it! Get creative, because there are no rules when it comes to tabletop design.

The burnt orange accents on the china and vintage Brno dining chairs inspired the color palette for my floral arrangement. I used a beautiful antique burl wood box that had been tucked away in Peter's studio to contain the flowers.

When it comes to giving flowers as a hostess gift, Peter and I agree that it is always best to present them in a vase filled with water. We have both had the awkward and challenging experience of trying to watch what's on the stove, answer the doorbell, open a bottle of wine, greet guests, light candles—and, in the middle of it all, get handed flowers that need to be trimmed and put into a vase with water. As a nice alternative to a bouquet of flowers, consider giving your hostess a great bottle of wine, a potted orchid, or a signed coffee-table book (such as *MAKE IT BEAUTIFUL*...hint hint).

Once the table was set, it was time to sit down and enjoy Peter's fantastic menu. The main course was Short Ribs with Parsnip Potatoes (see recipe on page 185) and a roasted beet salad with gorgonzola and green apples. After our delicious dinner, Peter generously packed up the leftovers for me to take home to my hungry husband—who was thrilled! Dinner at Chez Rosenbaum means the food, the wine, the design, and, most importantly, the company will be divine. After all, Chez Rosenbaum is my favorite restaurant in Chicago, too! ◆

Lining home décor fabrics with a soft cotton fabric is a great way to create customized dinner napkins that will match beautifully with your home's existing interior designs.

Nothing is more special than dining in a small space such as a library. Books are a beautiful backdrop for any dinner party.

Be creative and think outside of the box when it comes to choosing the right floral containers. If it can hold water, it can hold flowers. Look for containers that are about six to eight inches tall to ensure your centerpiece's finished height doesn't exceed eighteen inches.

Gingerbread House Decorating Party

Ho, Ho, Ho! Happy Holidays

A PARTY DEDICATED TO DECORATING gingerbread houses is a great idea for many reasons. It's a wonderful tradition to share with family and friends for the holidays. It's fun for all ages. It can be done easily on a budget. It encourages guests to be creative while they're having fun. Best of all, it's the perfect excuse to eat lots of candy! ¶ Having decorated many gingerbread houses in years past with the help of my mom, I knew I could pull this party together in my sleep. My special guest list consisted of my close friend, Kim Bartuch, and her beautiful children: Max, Madison, and Jack. ¶ My first stop was to my local bakery, where I placed an order for five undecorated gingerbread houses. Before placing the order, I researched images of gingerbread houses on the Internet, printed out a design I liked, and included the photo with my order.

Buying prebaked gingerbread house kits is another great way to go for this part of the process.

To cover the table, I chose a festive cotton velvet fabric. The fabric looked great and protected the table beautifully. Using a tableskirt at your gingerbread house decorating party will help quiet your darkest OCD moments—no matter how tempting it might be, cleaning the table during the decorating process is a no-no! Surrendering to the mess is so much more fun. Here's the good news: All that mess on the table is made of sugar, so it cleans up easily with warm water.

I picked up the candy, pastry bags, a dozen red roses, and ingredients for the Royal Icing (see recipe on page 187) at the grocery store and also purchased a variety of small, inexpensive holiday accessories from a craft store. Each sheet of Styrofoam used as a base for the houses should be close to an inch thick, so it can bear the weight of the house and still be covered easily with ribbon.

TIME TO PARTY!

The party's menu included milk, cookies, and a signature drink. To save myself some time, I bought decorated holiday cookies at the same bakery that made the gingerbread houses and dressed them up with holiday ribbon. The signature drink for the party—lovingly referred to as Mrs. Pedersen's Hot Cocoa (see recipe page 187) by Max, Madison, and Jack—was hot chocolate made from scratch on the stove. The kids especially loved the little felt "Ho" accents that topped the whipped cream in each child's cup.

As for putting the tablescape together, I did what I always do during the holidays: First, I pull out all my favorite holiday accessories. Then, I edit them ruthlessly! Since the Dromoland tableskirt was so festive on its own, it took a minimum of accessorizing to get the holiday look I wanted. A small arrangement of roses, holiday dinnerware, red glass votive candles, and the gingerbread houses themselves finished the look.

Once the kids arrived, things really got rolling. The kids were knocked out by the houses, the candy on the table, and their individual bowls of icing and pastry bags. The thrill was that each child had his or her own house to decorate, marked by a place card.

We were sad for the party to end, but we had lots of fun memories and great gingerbread houses to take with us! From this year forward, the Gingerbread House Decorating Party will join our list of holiday traditions. ✦

HERE'S A LITTLE TALE FROM BEHIND THE SCENES:

Gingerbread houses aren't just for kids! As I was setting up for the party, I decided to quickly decorate one of the houses to help get the kids excited and to give them inspiration. I was having fun doing my thing when my photographer, Peter Rosenbaum, a man with a long history of gently nudging me aside during projects and jumping in himself (the beautiful pink satin mini bow ties on the menu cards for the black-and-white baby shower were his

doing) did it again! Peter set down his camera and muscled his way into my gingerbread house decorating. Fortunately, I'm used to this kind of behavior; after all, I was raised by the Queen of Crafts. Miraculously, Peter and I finished wrestling over the pastry bag and completed the house just as the kids walked in to the kitchen. Note to self: In the future, always have an extra gingerbread house available for Peter and his assistant, Derick, to decorate!

Mixing doll house accessories with accents made of candy adds a fun dimension to the overall look and eliminates the frustration of crafting these items out of candy.

I use an inch-thick board made of Styrofoam
as a base for my gingerbread houses. In addition to
stabilizing the house and making it easier to carry,
it also provides a great platform for decorating.
Once I'm finished decorating the house, I coat the
Styrofoam with Royal Icing "snow," which adds
a festive holiday look to the house's yard. As a
finishing touch, I cover the edges of the Styrofoam
board with an inch-wide ribbon.

Provide each guest with a bowl of warm water and a washcloth to avoid the hassle of going back and forth to the sink to wash sticky hands.

Finishing
on the
18th Hole

WHISTLING STRAITS, KOHLER, WISCONSIN

Monica
3

Fore! My Husband

INISHING ON THE EIGHTEENTH HOLE—LITERALLY, as this was the last shoot for this book—was a gathering that started out as pure fantasy. During many of my challenging rounds of beginning golf, I made it to the eighteenth hole with my husband, Erik, and fantasized about just sitting down before the round was over to enjoy the gorgeous setting before my golf game would, again, get in the way. Since I had one special party left to plan, I had the perfect reason to try to make this fantasy come true. ❡ All the work for this book was coming to an end, but there was still one person I wanted to plan something very special for—Erik. Because golf is the way to Erik's heart, I knew I could make a special, memorable day for the two of us at one of our favorite places—Kohler, Wisconsin. ❡ Kohler is a destination where everything I am passionate about

Mixing the large-scale chairs with a smaller round table added to the magical look of setting up on the eighteenth-hole tee.

comes together. In the world of interior design, the Kohler Co. has long stood for high-end design, quality, and excellence. In the world of golf, Kohler's facilities are nothing short of world class. One of the property's Pete Dye-designed courses, Whistling Straits, has hosted two PGA Championships—the 2007 U.S. Senior Open and the 2005 Palmer Cup. In the future, the course will also host the 2015 PGA Championship and the 2020 Ryder Cup. The 2012 U.S. Women's Open will be held at Blackwolf Run, one of Whistling Straits' sister courses.

Each year, Erik and I kick off the golf season by heading to Kohler to play golf with another couple. This tradition began long before I had started my career in design. During one of these trips, my friend and I received high praise from our caddy. He told us that he'd never caddied for women who could actually talk through their backswing and still hit the ball. We agreed that it's a pretty impressive skill to have!

After a few calls to my good friends at the Kohler Co., I had my fantasy location all locked up. Now, I just had to pull the look together. A shopping trip to one of my favorite stores in Chicago, Brimfield, produced the classic wing chairs in Black Watch plaid—the oldest and most popular of all the tartans. I found the fabulous table at Kohler's Baker Odds & Ends furniture store. Mixing the large-scale chairs with a smaller round table added to the magical look of setting up on the eighteenth-hole tee. (Moving indoor furniture outdoors is a fun way to add a bit of surprise to any outdoor party.) Although setting up a party on the eighteenth-hole tee at Whistling Straits is pure fantasy, you can easily copy the look in your own backyard for Father's Day, Mother's Day, a birthday, or in honor of a PGA or LPGA Tour event.

Accessorizing the table was simple, since golf style is all about traditional details that are easy to find—crystal, silver, plaid, golf memorabilia, and so on. I introduced my own

A pair of bag tags with the course's logo doubled as napkin rings. The porcelain sheep were featured to pay homage to the sheep that graze alongside the course.

version of a cut crystal trophy cup, something you see at just about every golf tournament, in the form of a Waterford crystal iced tea glasses. They were perfect for serving Arnold Palmers, a mix of iced tea and lemonade.

At the pro shop (the only shop my husband spends more time in than I do), I found a treasure trove of table accessories. A pair of bag tags with the course's logo doubled as napkin rings. I also snagged some golf books and other accessories to fill a miniature tee box on the table—the box was originally a divider taken from the inside of an antique wooden jewelry box. The porcelain sheep were featured to pay homage to the sheep that graze alongside Whistling Straits and another sister course, the Irish Course.

For the place settings, I mixed solid cream and black printed dinnerware with cream-colored linen napkins to match the bag tag napkin rings. The short crystal candleholders held monogrammed golf balls that worked beautifully as place cards—a trick Erik marveled over. I showed my sense of humor with the score cards, which of course showed an even par.

We are still talking about the amazing time we had finishing on the eighteenth hole. For me, the day was a dream come true! ✦

I had a "Dye-abolical" designer moment while
trying to decide which spectacular view we
should feature when shooting the pictures:
the winding shoreline of Lake Michigan, or the
pure beauty of the eighteenth hole with the
magical clubhouse in the background. One day,
I hope to recreate this look for Herb Kohler
and Pete Dye, and let them decide the angle.

THE INTELLIGENT 🏌 GOLFER   UNIV

STRAIGHT DOWN THE MIDDLE   CHRONICLE BOOKS

EAM GOLF   GOODWIN

Don't think twice about moving
indoor furniture outdoors.
It is a great way to add surprise
and comfort to any outdoor party.
This look can easily be copied
in your own backyard for Father's Day,
Mother's Day, a birthday, or in honor
of a PGA or LPGA Tour event.

Recipes

Classic Bruschetta

BLACK AND WHITE BABY SHOWER *from Chef Khellil Abderezak at The Deer Path Inn*

1 pound (454 g) diced grape tomatoes

1 cup (24 g) hand-torn fresh basil

4 tablespoons (59 mL) extra virgin olive oil

Sea salt and freshly ground black pepper, to taste

1 large loaf rustic bread, sliced into inch-thick (2.5-cm) slices (about 24)

3 cloves peeled garlic, halved

Extra virgin olive oil, for drizzling

1. Preheat the oven to 350°F (180°C).

2. In a large mixing bowl, mix together the tomatoes and basil. Drizzle on the olive oil and continue to mix thoroughly. Season with the salt and pepper to taste. Set aside.

3. Rub the bread slices with the garlic clove halves. Place the bread slices on two baking sheets lined with parchment paper and toast them for 10 to 15 minutes, until golden brown. Remove the slices from the oven and set on platters to cool.

4. Top the bread slices with the tomato-basil mixture. Serve.

Grilled Chicken Salad with Pears, Gorgonzola, and Balsamic Vinegar

BLACK AND WHITE BABY SHOWER *from Chef Khellil Abderezak at The Deer Path Inn*

2 cups (228 g) chopped walnuts

1½ cups (356 mL) honey (divided)

½ cup (227 g) melted butter

Fresh thyme, to taste

4 (8-ounce [227-g]) boneless, skinless chicken breasts marinated in olive oil, fresh thyme, fresh rosemary, and minced garlic

4 Bartlett pears, sliced in half

1 cup (237 mL) extra virgin olive oil

½ cup (119 mL) balsamic vinegar

Salt and freshly ground black pepper, to taste

1 pound (454 g) mixed greens

4 ounces (114 g) gorgonzola cheese crumbles

1. Preheat the oven to 375°F (190°C).

2. Place the walnuts in a skillet over medium heat. After the skillet becomes hot, add ½ cup (119 mL) of the honey to the skillet. Shake the skillet frequently and continue to heat the walnuts until they become aromatic and take on a dark color. After 4 to 6 minutes, set them aside to cool.

3. In a small mixing bowl, combine the butter, the rest of the honey, and the fresh thyme. Place the pears in the bowl and mix well.

4. Place the pears on a baking sheet lined with parchment paper and bake them in the oven for 50 to 60 minutes, stirring them every 15 minutes. Remove the pears when they have evenly browned and allow them to cool.

5. While the pears are baking, on a very hot grill, grill the chicken breasts for 8 minutes on each side. Remove them from the grill to cool and then slice them into bite-sized pieces.

6. To make the dressing, pour the olive oil and balsamic vinegar into a blender and blend thoroughly, adding salt and pepper to taste.

7. Toss the mixed greens with the dressing and grilled chicken pieces. Add the pears, walnuts, and cheese to the serving bowl and toss thoroughly. Serve.

Asparagus Salad with a Confetti of Sweet Peppers

ECO-FRIENDLY GRADUATION PARTY *from Peggy Markel of Peggy Markel's Culinary Adventures (www.peggymarkel.com)*

3 bunches asparagus, ends peeled and trimmed

1 bunch fresh sage

¼ cup (59 mL) extra virgin olive oil

Coarse sea salt, to taste

2 each red and yellow peppers, julienned

2 small red onions, thinly sliced

2 baskets cherry tomatoes, halved

Tarragon Dressing, for drizzling (recipe follows)

1. Wash the asparagus. Bring a pot of salted water to a boil and blanch the asparagus in the water until it turns bright green, about 3 to 5 minutes, depending on size. Remove from the heat and drain.

2. In a small skillet, heat the olive oil on medium-high heat. Fry the sage in the oil for 2 to 3 seconds. Remove the sage from the skillet and transfer it to a paper towel. Sprinkle with the sea salt.

3. Place the asparagus on a platter. Scatter the red and yellow peppers, the onion, and the cherry tomatoes over the asparagus. Sprinkle with the sea salt.

4. Drizzle with the Tarragon Dressing and garnish with the fried sage. Serve.

Tarragon Dressing

ECO-FRIENDLY GRADUATION PARTY *from Peggy Markel of Peggy Markel's Culinary Adventures (www.peggymarkel.com)*

¼ cup (59 mL) extra virgin olive oil

1 shallot, minced

1 teaspoon dried tarragon

¼ teaspoon Dijon mustard

1 tablespoon fresh lemon juice

Sea salt and freshly ground black pepper, to taste

1. In a small bowl, whisk together all the ingredients, except the salt and pepper. Season to taste with the salt and pepper.

Baby New Potatoes with Fresh Rosemary

ECO-FRIENDLY GRADUATION PARTY *from Peggy Markel of Peggy Markel's Culinary Adventures (www.peggymarkel.com)*

16 baby red new potatoes, halved, roasted, and cooled

½ cup (119 mL) extra virgin olive oil

3 cloves garlic, peeled and finely chopped

Sea salt and freshly ground black pepper, to taste

2 sprigs fresh rosemary, coarsely chopped

1. Place the roasted potatoes in a bowl. Drizzle with the olive oil. Scatter the garlic over the potatoes. Season to taste with the salt and pepper.

2. Add the chopped rosemary and toss together. Transfer to a platter and serve.

Roasted Organic Chicken with Aromatic Salt

ECO-FRIENDLY GRADUATION PARTY *from Peggy Markel of Peggy Markel's Culinary Adventures (www.peggymarkel.com)*

AROMATIC SALT:

2 stalks each fresh rosemary and thyme

¼ bunch fresh sage

1 fresh bay leaf

2 cloves garlic

3 tablespoons (55 g) coarse sea salt

CHICKEN:

1 whole (3½ lbs. [1.60 kg]) free-range organic chicken

1 lemon, cut in half

2 stalks rosemary, left whole

Extra virgin olive oil, for drizzling

Coarse sea salt and freshly ground black pepper

1. Preheat the oven to 425°F (220°C).

2. To make the aromatic salt, finely chop the rosemary, thyme, sage, bay leaf, and garlic and mix together with the salt. Set aside.

3. Discard the internal organs packed inside the chicken, if included. Pat the chicken dry. Rub the outside of the chicken with the olive oil and sprinkle the cavity of the chicken with the sea salt and pepper. Tie the chicken's legs together with kitchen twine to help it keep its shape and cook more evenly.

4. Rub the aromatic salt all over the outside of the chicken and in the folds of the wings. Place the chicken in a roasting pan and roast the chicken for 25 to 30 minutes.

5. Remove the chicken from the oven and baste it with the pan juices. Return to the chicken to the oven, reduce the temperature to 375°F (190°C) and roast for another 30 to 40 minutes, basting once or twice, until the juices run clear when a knife is pierced into the chicken's thigh or a meat thermometer inserted deep into the chicken's breast reaches 165°F (74°C). Cover and let rest for 5 minutes before carving.

Orzo Salad

ECO-FRIENDLY GRADUATION PARTY *from Peggy Markel of Peggy Markel's Culinary Adventures (www.peggymarkel.com)*

1½ cups (270 g) orzo pasta

1 bunch fresh basil, chiffonaded

1 (4-ounce [114 g]) container feta cheese

2 cloves garlic, chopped

Sea salt and freshly ground black pepper, to taste

Lemon Parsley Dressing (recipe follows), for drizzling

Roasted lemon, for garnish

1. Bring a pot of water to a boil over high heat. Stir in the orzo. Cover the pot partially and cook, stirring frequently, until the orzo is tender but still firm to the bite, about 7 minutes. Drain the orzo and transfer it to a large, wide bowl. Toss until the orzo cools slightly. Set aside to cool completely.

2. Toss the orzo with the beans, tomatoes, onion, basil, feta cheese, and garlic. Season the mixture with the salt and pepper, to taste, and drizzle with the Lemon Parsley Dressing. Serve at room temperature with the roasted lemon as garnish.

....

Lemon Parsley Dressing

ECO-FRIENDLY GRADUATION PARTY *from Peggy Markel of Peggy Markel's Culinary Adventures (www.peggymarkel.com)*

  1 cup (237 mL) extra virgin olive oil

  ¼ cup (59 mL) fresh lemon juice

  ¼ bunch parsley, finely chopped

  2 teaspoons honey

  2 teaspoons salt

  ¾ teaspoon freshly ground black pepper

1. In a small bowl, whisk together all the ingredients, except the salt and pepper. Season to taste with the salt and pepper.

....

Lemon Squares

TEA FOR TWO *from my mom's kitchen*

CRUST:

  1 cup (227 g) melted butter

  ½ cup (50 g) powdered sugar

  2 cups (242 g) flour

FILLING:

  4 eggs

  2 cups (400 g) sugar

  6 tablespoons (89 mL) fresh lemon juice

  Confectioners' sugar, for sprinkling

1. Preheat the oven to 350°F (180°C).

2. In a large mixing bowl, mix together the crust ingredients. Once the ingredients are thoroughly mixed, press the mixture into the bottom of a greased 9 x 13-inch (22.5 x 32.5-cm) pan.

3. Bake for 20 minutes or until the crust is slightly browned. Remove the crust from the oven and set aside.

4. In a large mixing bowl, beat together the eggs, sugar, and lemon juice until thoroughly combined. Pour the mixture over the over the browned crust and bake for 25 minutes, or until firm. Remove from the oven and set the pan on a rack to cool.

5. Sprinkle with the confectioners' sugar. Slice into squares and serve.

....

Short Ribs Braised in Red Wine with Parsnip Potatoes

BOOK CLUB *from the kitchen of Peter Rosenbaum*

  ½ slab applewood smoked bacon

  ½ cup (119 mL) canola oil

  4–6 short ribs

  1 cup (121 g) flour

  2 large onions, chopped

  2 whole carrots

  2 ribs whole celery

  1 pound (454 g) sliced mushrooms (white or crimini)

  2 springs fresh thyme

  3 bay leaves

  1 bunch fresh parsley, chopped

  1 teaspoon salt

  2 tablespoons tomato paste

  1 bottle good red wine

  Fresh thyme, for garnish

1. Preheat the oven to 350°F (180°C).

2. Slice the bacon into small, thick "lardon"-sized pieces. Render the bacon over high heat in a heavy skillet. Remove the bacon from the skillet and set aside.

3. Add the canola oil to the bacon fat remaining in the skillet and heat the oil over medium heat.

4. With paper towels, thoroughly dry the short ribs. Dredge them in the flour, coating each piece evenly. Add the flour-coated ribs to the skillet and brown them thoroughly. Take care not to crowd the ribs in the skillet; if the skillet is not large enough, brown them in two batches.

5. In a large, heavy Dutch oven with a tight-fitted lid, place the onions, carrots, celery, mushrooms, and bacon. Arrange the ribs on top of the vegetables and add the thyme, bay leaves, parsley, and salt.

6. In a separate bowl, mix together the tomato paste and wine. Pour the mixture over the short ribs. The liquid should come up to the level of the short ribs but should not completely cover them. If there is not enough liquid, add more wine.

7. Cover with the lid and bake for 3 to 4 hours, until the ribs are very tender and separate easily from the bones.

8. Remove the ribs and vegetables from the Dutch oven. Strain the gravy, which should be a very rich brown-red and should be thickened, through a fat separator.

9. Strip the connective tissue and bones from the meat. Transfer the vegetables to a separate serving bowl. Serve the short ribs on a bed of Parsnip Potatoes (recipe follows) with a garnish of fresh thyme with lots of gravy.

······································

Parsnip Potatoes

BOOK CLUB *from the kitchen of Peter Rosenbaum*

3 pounds (1.36 kg) russet potatoes, peeled and cubed

1 pound (454 g) parsnips, peeled and cubed into smaller cubes than the potatoes

1 teaspoon salt

½ pound (227 g) butter

½ cup (119 mL) heavy cream

1. Add parsnips to boiling salted water. After 5 minutes, add the potatoes to the salted water. Continue boiling the parsnips and potatoes until they are soft and ready for mashing.

2. Mash the parsnips and potatoes by hand with the salt, butter, and cream.

3. Serve with the Short Ribs.

······································

Gnocchi di Patate

THAT'S ITALIAN *from Chef Fabio Viviani, Café Firenze (www.fabioviviani.com)*

3 medium peeled, roasted, and mashed potatoes, chilled

1 pinch salt

1 pinch freshly ground black pepper

½ teaspoon nutmeg

1 egg

2 cups (242 g) all-purpose flour, divided (or more as needed)

Extra virgin olive oil, for drizzling

1. In a large mixing bowl fitted with the paddle attachment, beat together the potatoes, salt, pepper, nutmeg, and egg.

2. Continue beating the mixture on low speed. Add the flour, ¼ cup (30 g) at a time, until thoroughly mixed (the mixture should be a large lump that sticks to the paddle). You should be able to rip off pieces of dough without your hands becoming so wet that the potato mixture sticks to them. If it is still sticky, add small amounts of additional flour until it reaches the desired consistency.

3. With generously floured hands, turn the dough onto a floured surface. Shape the dough into balls, using about 1 fist-sized piece for each ball.

4. Roll each ball with the palm of your hand into a cylindrical shape. Slice the cylinders into ¾-inch (2-cm) gnocchi dumplings.

5. Cook 20 to 30 of the gnocchi cylinders at a time in boiling water. Do not stir or mix the gnocchi as they boil. When the first 2 or 3 gnocchi float to the top of the water, remove all the gnocchi from the pot with a spider or slotted spoon and place them on a platter. Drizzle the gnocchi with the extra virgin olive oil and serve.

....

Mrs. Pedersen's Hot Cocoa

GINGERBREAD HOUSE DECORATING PARTY *from my very own kitchen*

½ cup (100 g) sugar

¼ cup (22 g) Hershey's unsweetened cocoa

Dash salt

⅓ cup (79 mL) hot water

1 quart (948 mL) milk

¾ teaspoon vanilla extract

Miniature marshmallows or sweetened whipped cream, if desired

1. Stir together the sugar, cocoa, and salt in a medium saucepan; stir in the water. Cook the mixture over medium heat, stirring constantly, until it comes to a boil. Continue boiling, stirring constantly, for 2 minutes.

2. Add the milk. Stirring constantly, continue heating until the cocoa reaches serving temperature. Do not boil.

3. Remove from the heat; add the vanilla. Beat the mixture with a rotary beater or whisk until foamy. Serve topped with marshmallows or whipped cream, if desired.

....

Royal Icing

GINGERBREAD HOUSE DECORATING PARTY *adapted from the book* The Secrets of Baking *by Sherry Yard*

4 cups (400 g) confectioners' sugar

3 tablespoons (30 g) meringue powder

½–¾ cup (119–178 mL) warm water

½ teaspoon vanilla extract

Food coloring, as desired

1. In a large mixing bowl, beat together the confectioners' sugar and meringue powder on low speed until combined. Add the water and food coloring, as desired, and beat on medium to high speed until very glossy and stiff peaks form (5 to 7 minutes). If necessary to get the right consistency, add more confectioners' sugar or water.

2. Use immediately as icing.

....

Potato Leek Soup

FINISHING ON THE 18TH HOLE *from the Clubhouse at Whistling Straits, Kohler, Wisconsin*

½ Spanish onion, julienned

2 cloves garlic, chopped

½ bunch leeks, whites only, julienned

¼ cup (57 g) butter, melted

¼ cup (59 mL) cream sherry

2 quarts (1.9 L) chicken stock

2 quarts (1.9 L) leek stock

5 pounds (2.27 kg) Yukon Gold potatoes, peeled and cubed

1 cup (237 mL) heavy cream

Roux, for thickening

Salt, white pepper, and Tabasco sauce, for seasoning

1. In a large Dutch oven over medium-high heat, sauté the onion, garlic, and leeks in the butter. Deglaze the Dutch oven with the cream sherry. Add the stocks and the potatoes to the Dutch oven, cover, and cook until the potatoes are soft.

2. Using an immersion blender, purée the mixture until smooth. Add the cream and thicken the mixture with the roux. Season to taste with the salt, white pepper, and Tabasco sauce.

Sources

All of the custom tableskirts and table linens for this book were made by Private Label Linens Chicago (www.privatelabellinens.com).

BLACK AND WHITE BABY SHOWER: LOCATION—Gail Plechaty, Real Simple Designs; FABRIC—Scalamandré (#16449-001); STEMWARE, DINNERWARE, FLATWARE—Crate & Barrel (www.crateandbarrel.com); MENU CARDS, PLACE CARDS RIBBON, ZEBRA STAMP, LETTERS—Paper Source (www.paper-source.com); CUSTOM CHALKBOARD, GRAPHIC DESIGNS, MENU PLACE CARDS—Kristin Korjenek, Flourish Designs (klkcreative@yahoo.com); CAKE—The Bent Fork (www.thebentfork.com); WINE—Seven Daughters Moscato

ECO-FRIENDLY GRADUATION PARTY: FABRIC—Scalamandré (#16242-007); RECIPES—Peggy Markel (www.peggymarkel.com); GLASS VOTIVES, FLORAL CONTAINERS—Partylite (www.partylite.com); SERVING PIECES—Ikea (www.ikea.com); DINNERWARE, STEMWARE, FLATWARE, TABLES—Hall's Rental (www.hallsrental.com); ANTIQUE CHANDELIERS—Antiquaire (www.antiquaireonline.com); TAPER CANDLES—Creative Candles (www.creativecandles.com); RED OAK SEEDLINGS—P. Clifford Miller Landscape Artistry (www.landscapeartistry.net); MENU CARDS, RIBBON, GUESTBOOK—Paper Source (www.paper-source.com); HEMSTITCH LINEN NAPKINS—Williams-Sonoma (www.williams-sonoma.com); CUSTOM CHALKBOARD AND MENU CARD—Kristin Korjenek, Flourish Designs (klkcreative@yahoo.com); WINES—Rutherford Hill Sauvignon Blanc and Rutherford Hill Merlot

THE PERFECT WEDDING: FABRIC—Scalamandré (#26531-003 and #36284-001); DINNERWARE, CHIAVARI CHAIRS, TABLES—Hall's Rental (www.hallsrental.com); STEMWARE—Ivy & Co. (www.ivyandco.net); SILVER CUPS, VOTIVES—Michaels (www.michaels.com); RIBBON, WRAPPING PAPER—Paper Source (www.paper-source.com); CAKE—The Bent Fork (www.thebentfork.com)

COFFEE AND...: STRIPED AND PAISLEY FABRICS—Calico Corners; CHINA AND TABLETOP ACCESSORIES—Peter Rosenbaum's personal collection; ACCENT PLATES—Pottery Barn (www.potterybarn.com)

TEA FOR TWO: FABRIC—Scalamandré (#16323-005); FLORAL CONTAINERS, ACCESSORIES—Ivy & Co. (www.ivyandco.net); ANTIQUE WOODEN BOX—The Find Antiques (www.thefindantiques.com)

WINE AND DESIGN: WOODEN TRAYS, IRON CANDLESTICKS, FLATWARE, CORKSCREWS—Pottery Barn (www.potterybarn.com); LEATHER WINE JOURNALS, VOTIVES, SILVER CUPS, WOODEN CHEESE TRAY—Michaels (www.michaels.com); CHEDDAR CHEESES—Kerrygold Cheese; RIEDEL WINE GLASSES—Bed Bath & Beyond (www.bedbathandbeyond.com); HEMSTITCH LINEN NAPKINS, HORN-HANDLED CHEESE KNIVES—Williams-Sonoma (www.williams-sonoma.com); SLIP COVERED CHAIRS—Real Simple Designs; WINES—A variety of wines from Stags Leap District, Napa Valley, CA (www.stagsleapdistrict.com)

THAT'S ITALIAN: FABRIC—Scalamandré (#16292-003); TABLETOP ACCESSORIES, CHINA, AND FLATWARE—Omega Cinema Props (www.omegacinemaprops.com); WINES—Santa Margherita Chianti Classico Riserva and Santa Margherita Pinot Grigio

BOOK CLUB: FABRIC—Scalamandré (#16316-003); CUSTOM NAPKINS—Private Label Linens Chicago (www.privatelabellinens.com); TABLETOP ACCESSORIES—Peter Rosenbaum's personal collection; WINES—Chimney Rock Cabernet Sauvignon

GINGERBREAD HOUSE DECORATING PARTY: FABRIC—Scalamandré (#16357-003); RIBBONS—Michaels (www.michaels.com); DINNERWARE, FLORAL VASE—Crate & Barrel (www.crateandbarrel.com); GINGERBREAD HOUSES—The Bent Fork (www.thebentfork.com); RED GLASS PLACE CARD HOLDERS—Partylite (www.partylite.com); RED IRON LANTERNS—Pier1 Imports (www.pier1.com)

FINISHING ON THE 18TH HOLE: CHAIRS, PILLOW, BLANKET—Brimfield (www.brimfieldus.com); MILLING ROAD COLLECTION TABLE—Baker Furniture at Kohler Interiors (www.kohlerinteriors.com); BOOKS, GOLF ACCESSORIES—Kohler at Home (www.kohlerathome.com); WATERFORD CRYSTAL GLASSES—Macy's (www.macys.com); DINNERWARE—Peachtree Place (www.peachtreeplaceonline.com); FLATWARE—Crate & Barrel (www.crateandbarrel.com); HEMSTITCH LINEN NAPKINS—Williams-Sonoma (www.williams-sonoma.com)

Acknowledgments

I WOULD NEVER HAVE BEEN ABLE TO DO THIS BOOK without the encouragement of my friends **Susan Holmer** and **Peter Rosenbaum**. Susan, your enthusiasm for my work is humbling, and your ability to give me courage is a treasure. Peter, you gave so generously of yourself: your time, your limitless talents, and your friendship. You elevate my work to a whole new level. I could never have taken on this project, if not for you. If I had a tattoo, it would have your name on it in a heart. I owe you the most sincere thanks!

I also give thanks:

To **Lou Renzo**, **Dan Casper**, and **Peter Julian** at **Scalamandré**, for delivering bolts and bolts of beautiful fabrics to my front door. It all started with Scalamandré!

To **Gail Plechaty**, who opened her home and shared her beautiful daughters, **Charlotte** and **Sophia**, with me for this project. A location scout is born! Your early morning calls for coffee got me through many tough days. Thank you!

To **Bill Merryfield**, for bringing his endless talent to long shoot days. I am so fortunate that America's friend **Sally Thompson** and **Pat Handler** share you with me.

To **David Simmons** and **Andre Walker**, for designing my favorite tableskirt of all time.

To **Richard Schneider** and **Delma Zia** at **Private Label Linens**, for sewing the beautiful and speedy tableskirts you see on these pages.

To **Derick Smith**, for working so very hard and for being a lighting genius!

To **Todd Stone**, for stepping in as photographer so Peter could try Fabio's delicious gnocchi.

To **Marty Sorenson**, for doing such a great job in post-production.

To **Fabio Viviani**, for making the time to participate in this project and generously opening his restaurant to me. It's no accident that you are America's fan favorite! You need your own show!

To **Joyce Elven** at **Partylite**, for filling my car with beautiful accessories and turning a one-day job into a memorable weekend for my mom and me.

To **John Terlato** and the marketing team at Rutherford Hill, for allowing me to bring Rutherford Hill to my table.

To **Antonio Ballatore** and **Bethany Dick** for being the perfect guests. Café Firenze was so much fun.

To **Todd Weber**, **Lauren Aust**, **Dirk Willis**, and all of my friends at **Kohler Co.**, for making my Whistling Straits dream come true.

To **Doug Seibold**, **Perrin Davis**, and **Al Brandtner** at **Agate Publishing**, for getting behind *Make It Beautiful*.

To **Loren Ruch** at **HGTV**, for being such a positive force in my life. The only thing missing from this book is you, **Dolly**, **Ali Booker**, a cute party for **Bill Myers**' twins, and **Shawn Visco**'s friends.

To **Kathleen Finch**, for bringing a woman's touch to **HGTV**.

To **Leslie Weiner**, **Melanie Pott**, and **Becky McCallum**, for being the most wonderful design team. I miss you guys every day.

To **Rachel Handler**, **Stephanie Lentz**, and **Lisa Goldman**, for sharing wine and design.

To **Phyllis Carlucci** and **Luigi Negroni**, for teaching me so much about fine dining, presentation, and perfect friendship.

To **Peggy Markel**, for the graduation party's fabulous recipes. A *Peggy Markel Culinary Adventure* is definitely on my to-do list!

To **Eleanor Simon**, **Liza Cruzat Brooks**, and **Shannon Willford**, for participating in my special project. I miss you guys so much!

To **Beth Peterson**, for doing such a great job.

To **Anne Matthews**, **Anastasia Livaditis**, and **Tracey Hamilton**—having your friendship is the perfect decoration.

To my **wonderful fans**, for not turning the channel!

And especially, to my husband **Erik**, who picks me up when I am tired, never stops making me laugh, and patiently listens to my nonstop chatter. You make my life more beautiful. xo

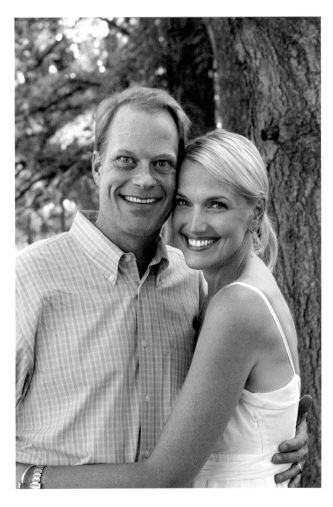

For more ways to make it beautiful, visit www.monicapedersen.com.